News for every day of the year

A British soldier kisses a baby in front of cheering crowds following the Liberation of Paris, 26 August 1944.

By Hugh Morrison

MONTPELIER PUBLISHING

Front cover (clockwise from left):
British troops in Rome following its liberation on 4 June.
Poster for the film *National Velvet*, released on 14 December
Crowds embrace British troops after the liberation of Paris, 25 August.
The German Me63 rocket fighter plane, launched on 28 July.
Allied troops land on the Normandy beaches on D-Day, 6 June.

Back cover (clockwise from top):
Children lay flowers in newly liberated Paris on Bastille Day, 14 July.
US President Franklin D Roosevelt is elected for a historic fourth term on 7 November.
The German V2 rocket, first launched against Britain on 8 September.
British Prime Minister Winston Churchill meets Free French leader General de Gaulle in Morocco, 12 January.
Poster for the film *Gaslight,* released on 5 May.
Band leader Glenn Miller, who goes missing on 15 December.
A British military postman in partially liberated Holland, November 1944.

Published in Great Britain by Montpelier Publishing.
Printed and distributed by Amazon KDP.
This edition © 2023. All rights reserved.

ISBN: 9798385742523

January 1944

Saturday 1: 421 RAF bombers raid Berlin by night.

The architect Edwin Lutyens dies aged 74.

Sunday 2: Allied troops land successfully on the Pacific island of Papua New Guinea in Operation Dexterity.

Betty Smith's novel *A Tree Grows in Brooklyn* tops the New York Times bestseller list.

Monday 3: Berlin's Reichschancellery is hit in an RAF bombing raid.

Soviet troops take Olevsk, bringing them to within 10 miles of the Polish border.

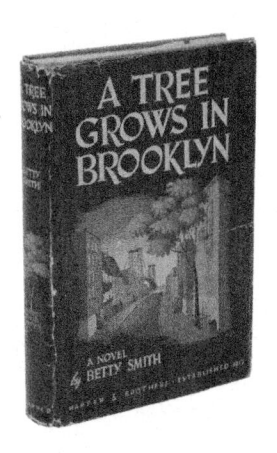

A Tree Grows in Brooklyn tops the *New York Times* bestseller list on 2 January.

Tuesday 4: The German government announces the mobilisation of schoolchildren for military purposes. By the end of the war in 1945, children as young as 8 are reported to be assisting in artillery posts.

Wednesday 5: As Soviet forces prepare to cross the Polish border, Poland's government in exile issues a formal statement that it, not the Soviets, has the only rightful claim to rule the country.

January 1944

Thursday 6: Soviet forces cross into Poland, capturing the town of Rokitno.

Friday 7: US troops capture the town of San Vittore del Lazio as the Allies push further north into German-occupied Italy.

Saturday 8: Show trials begin in German-occupied Italy of those in government accused of voting for Benito Mussolini's removal from power.

Sunday 9: The guitarist and songwriter Jimmy Page of Led Zeppelin is born in Heston, Middlesex.

Jimmy Page is born on 9 January.

Monday 10: Five Italians are sentenced to death for voting to remove Benito Mussolini from power.

Tuesday 11: The Soviet Union refutes the Polish government-in-exile's statement of 5 January, and claims it has sole authority over Poland.

The Alfred Hitchcock-directed film *Lifeboat* is released.

Wednesday 12: Britain's Prime Minister Winston Churchill and Free French leader Charles de Gaulle meet in Morocco to discuss French involvement in the opening of the Second Front (D-Day).

The boxer Joe Frazier is born in Beaufort, South Carolina (died 2011).

Thursday 13: US forces in Allied-occupied Italy warn

Left: Churchill and De Gaulle meet in Morocco on 12 January.

January 1944

Two girls assemble sub-machine guns during the Siege of Leningrad, which ends on 27 January.

Joe Frazier is born on 12 January.

of a growing typhus epidemic.

Friday 14: Soviet leader Joseph Stalin begins the Leningrad-Novgorod Offensive, the first of his 'Ten Blows' against the Axis' Eastern Front.

Saturday 15: 10,000 die in an earthquake in San Juan province, Argentina.

Sunday 16: Dwight D. Eisenhower takes up his role as supreme commander of the Allied Expeditionary Forces.

Monday 17: The Battle of Monte Cassino begins in Italy.

Meat rationing is introduced in Australia.

Tuesday 18: Soviet forces make the first small breakthrough in the two-year-long Siege of Leningrad; the siege ends on 27 January.

Wednesday 19: The RAF carries out its heaviest bombing raid of the war so far on Berlin, dropping 2300 tons of high explosive in half an hour.

Thursday 20: Winston Churchill meets with the Polish government-in-exile, pushing for compromise with the Soviet forces liberating the country from German occupation. He suggests the partition of Poland into two states.

January 1944

Edvard Munch (inset) dies on 23 January. He is best known for his painting *The Scream* (above).

Friday 21: The Luftwaffe begins Operation Steinbock, (also known as the Baby Blitz), a series of major bombing raids on southern England.

The short-lived Jesselton Revolt, an uprising in North Borneo, is put down by Japanese occupying forces.

Saturday 22: The Battle of Anzio begins in Italy as Allied forces make coastal landings in an attempt to out-flank occupying German forces.

Sunday 23: HMS *Janus* is sunk off the Italian coast by a German Fritz-X glide bomb (a prototype 'drone').

The Norwegian painter Edvard Munch dies aged 80.

Actor Rutger Hauer is born in Breukelen, Netherlands. (died 2019).

Monday 24: 96 die when the British hospital ship *St David* is bombed off the Italian coast.

Tuesday 25: The Japanese destroyer *Suzukaze* is sunk by the USS *Skipjack* in Micronesia.

Wednesday 26: Argentina breaks off diplomatic relations with the Axis powers.

Left: A Fritz-X glide bomb of the type which sinks HMS *Janus* on 23 January.

January 1944

Thursday 27: The Siege of Leningrad ends.

Friday 28: The British government warns Joseph Stalin that the establishment of Soviet rule in occupied Poland will 'preclude agreement' among the Allies.

Saturday 29: HMS *Spartan* is sunk off the coast of Anzio by a German glide bomb.

Sunday 30: The British 5th division breaks through the Gustav Line, one of the principal defences of German-occupied Italy.

A mushroom cloud formed by the explosion of a Japanese arms dump on an atoll during the Battle of Kwajalein, 31 January.

Monday 31: The Battle of Kwajalein begins in the Marshall Islands.

February 1944

Tuesday 1: All French resistance forces are unified as the French Forces of the Interior (FFI), to act under the orders of the Allies following the opening of the Second Front (D-Day).

Wednesday 2: The Battle of Narva begins on the Eastern Front.

Thursday 3: German forces counter-attack at Anzio in Italy, sealing off the Allied bridgehead.

Friday 4: The German submarine U-854 is sunk in the Baltic Sea.

Saturday 5: The Battle of the Admin Box begins in Burma.

Left: a senior German officer inspects soldiers of Italy's Axis forces during the Anzio counter-offensive, which begins on 3 February.

February 1944

Sunday 6: Soviet bombers attack the Finnish capital, Helsinki, in the city's largest raid of the war.

Monday 7: US President Roosevelt asks the Polish government-in-exile to accept the partition compromise with the USSR proposed by Winston Churchill.

Tuesday 8: 2670 Italian prisoners of war are killed when the German prison ship *Petrella* is sunk; meanwhile 2765 Japanese perish when the *Lima Maru* is sunk in the East China Sea.

The Bishop of Chichester.

Actor Roger Lloyd Pack (Trigger in *Only Fools and Horses*) is born in London (died 2014).

Wednesday 9: The Bishop of Chichester, George Bell, sparks controversy when he speaks out against the indiscriminate bombing of German civilians by Allied forces.

Thursday 10: Amphibious Allied forces land successfully at Saidor, New Guinea.

PAYE (Pay As You Earn) taxation is introduced in the UK.

Friday 11: Soviet forces re-capture Shepetovka in the Ukraine.

Left: German troops survey bomb damage during the Battle of Narva, which begins on 2 February.

February 1944

Above: Jerry Springer is born on 13 February.

Saturday 12: 4000 Italian POWs are killed when the German prison ship *Oria* sinks in a storm in the eastern Mediterranean.

1297 die when the SS *Khedive Ismail*, a British troopship, is torpedoed byy a Japanese submarine in the Indian Ocean.

Sunday 13: Actress Stockard Channing (*Saturday Night Fever*) is born in New York City.

TV presenter Jerry Springer is born in London, England.

Monday 14: The USA declares neutrality in the border dispute between Poland and the USSR.

Tuesday 15: The Battle of the Green Islands begins in the Pacific; New Zealand forces capture the islands from the Japanese five days later.

An exhausted US marine, aged just 19, at the end of the Battle of Eniwetok on 23 February.

Wednesday 16: Following another devastating Allied air-raid on Berlin, German propaganda minister Goebbels takes the unusual step of exaggerating the damage caused, in the hope that the city is no longer considered a worthwhile target.

The war film *Passage to Marseille* starring Humphrey Bogart is released.

Thursday 17: The Battle of Karavia Bay begins off the island of New Britain in the Pacific.

Friday 18: In Operation Jericho, 258 prisoners escape from

February 1944

Amiens prison in France following an Allied air raid which destroys the prison wall.

Saturday 19: In the 'Baby Blitz', 187 German bombers attack London in the worst raid since 1941.

Sunday 20: The Allies launch 'Big Week', a concentrated series of air raids intended to knock out German aircraft manufacture.

Monday 21: General Hideki Tojo, Prime Minister of Japan, becomes Chief of Staff of the Japanese army.

General Tojo takes over the Japanese army on 21 February.

Tuesday 22: Britain's Prime Minister Winston Churchill makes a speech in the House of Commons in which he states Britain had never guaranteed Poland's borders, claiming the Soviet demands for Polish territory are 'reasonable'.

Wednesday 23: The Battle of Eniwetok ends in US victory.

US Marine pilots take a break from combat during the Battle of the Green Islands, which ends on 27 February.

February 1944

Thursday 24: Edwin Linkomies, Prime Minister of Finland, announces his country is ready to change sides and support the Allies.

Friday 25: Iceland declares independence from Denmark.

Queen Wilhelmina of the Netherlands, in exile in London, narrowly escapes death when her home is bombed.

Saturday 26: The Polish government-in-exile formally rejects Churchill's compromise plan to cede part of Poland to the USSR.

Sunday 27: The Battle of the Green Islands ends in Allied victory.

Monday 28: The First Narva Offensive ends in German victory.

Tuesday 29: Free French naval forces engage with the German navy in the Battle of Ist in the Adriatic.

March 1944

Wednesday 1: Adolf Hitler meets with the puppet-government leaders of the Independent State of Croatia.

Singer Roger Daltrey of The Who is born in Hammersmith, London.

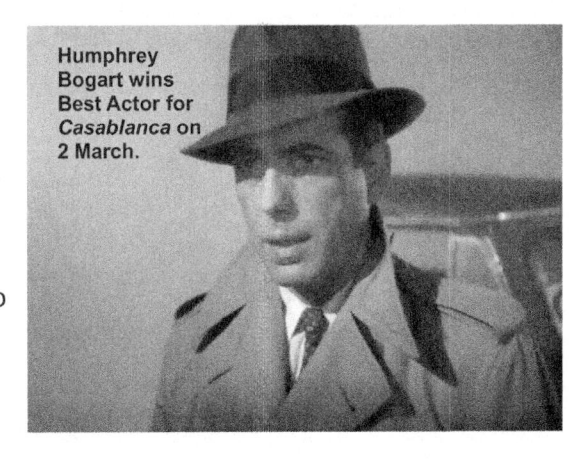

Humphrey Bogart wins Best Actor for *Casablanca* on 2 March.

Thursday 2: *Casablanca* wins Best Picture in the 16th Academy Awards.

Friday 3: Joseph Stalin rejects British proposals for the settlement of the Polish/Soviet border.

Saturday 4: *Besame Mucho* by Jimmy Dorsey and his Orchestra hits number one in the US charts.

Sunday 5: The 77th Indian Infantry Brigade (the Chindits) are flown into Burma by glider in Operation Thursday. The Chindits are the first military unit to fight with a supply chain solely from the air.

March 1944

Monday 6: The first major Allied daylight bombing raid on Berlin takes place.

Opera singer Kiri Te Kanawa is born in Gisborne, New Zealand.

Tuesday 7: The Japanese launch Operation U-Go, the invasion of India.

Wednesday 8: The Battle of Imphal, the first major Japanese attack on India begins.

Thursday 9: Desperate German counter-attacks take place as Soviet troops reach the border of Romania.

Friday 10: A temporary stalemate is reached on the Italian Front as troops are bogged down in mud at Anzio.

Women teachers in Britain are no longer required to give up work upon marriage.

Men of the Devonshire Regiment sign a Japanese flag captured during the Battle of Imphal, which begins on 8 March.

Saturday 11: Senior German officer Eberhard von Breitenbruch fails in a planned attempt to assassinate Adolf Hitler, when he is barred from meeting with him at the last moment.

French police discover the remains of ten murder victims in tthe home of a doctor, Marcel Petiot. He is executed in 1946.

Sunday 12: Hitler orders Operation Margarethe, the occupation of Hungary.

Monday 13: The Soviet army captures the city of Kherson in the Ukraine.

March 1944

Left: Soviet troops cross the River Dnieper to capture the Ukrainian city of Kherson from the German army on 13 March.

Tuesday 14: Winston Churchill announces a clampdown on the leaking of secrets to the Axis via neutral Eire.

Wednesday 15: Despite following a devastating artillery barrage, an Allied infantry attack on Monte Cassino in Italy is repulsed.

The State Anthem of the Soviet Union replaces the communist *Internationale* as the USSR's national anthem.

Thursday 16: The Japanese destroyer *Shirakumo* is sunk by the USS Tautog off the coast of Hokkaido.

Friday 17: 26 die and 88 US aircraft are destroyed when Italy's Mount Vesuvius erupts.

The model Patti Boyd is born in Taunton, Somerset.

Saturday 18: Admiral Miklos Horthy, Regent of Hungary, meets with Hitler in Austria to discuss the terms of his country's occupation by Germany.

Left: Kiri te Kanawa is born on 6 March.

March 1944

Sunday 19: Hungary is occupied by eight German divisions in order to prevent its government making peace with the USSR.

Monday 20: Japanese forces attempt to invade India at Shangshak but are pushed back by the Indian Army under Lt Gen Geoffry Scoones.

Tuesday 21: The Finnish government secretly agrees to reject peace terms offered by the USSR.

Wednesday 22: Occupying German forces in Hungary order all Jewish businesses to close, and a round-up of Jews begins.

80 US bombers are destroyed as the eruption of Italy's Mount Vesuvius continues.

Lt Gen Geoffry Scoones, Indian Army, leads the push back against the Japanese on 20 March.

Thursday 23: Allied forces withdraw from the assault on Monte Cassino, Italy.

Above: one of the 80 USAF bomber planes destroyed by the eruption of Mount Vesuvius on 22 March.

March 1944

Diana Ross is born on 26 March.

The romantic comedy film *The Heavenly Body* starring William Powell and Hedy Lamarr is released in the USA.

Friday 24: 76 Royal Air Force POWs break out of the German prison camp Stalag Luft III in what becomes known as the Great Escape.

RAF Flight Sergeant Nicholas Alkemade survives a fall of 18,000 feet (5486m) after bailing out of a burning Lancaster bomber over Germany. He is unable to use his parachute due to it having caught fire; miraculously his fall is broken by pine branches and snowdrifts and he escapes with minor injuries, spending the remainder of the war in a POW camp.

Saturday 25: A furious Adolf Hitler orders the execution of any escapees from Stalag Luft III who are recaptured. Soon afterwards, 73 of the 76 are caught and 50 shot. Following a post-war RAF Police investigation into the case, 21 German soldiers held responsible are executed.

Sunday 26: Singer Diana Ross is born in Detroit, Michigan.

Monday 27: The Finnish government meets with Soviet representatives to discuss peace terms.

Tuesday 28: Britain's Parliament votes to award equal pay for men and women teachers.

Wednesday 29: Soviet forces take the city of Kolomea, Ukraine.

Thursday 30: The RAF suffers its worst loss of the war as 96 planes are shot down over Nuremberg.

Friday 31: Admiral Mineichi Koga, commander in chief of the Japanese navy, is killed in a plane crash during bad weather off the coast of the Philippines.

April 1944

Saturday 1: Civilians are banned from going within ten miles of England's south coast as D-Day preparations begin.

Sunday 2: Soviet forces enter Romania.

A failed uprising takes place against the rule of Maximiliano Hernandez Martinez in El Salvador.

Monday 3: Singer Tony Orlando is born in New York City.

The Royal Navy carries out an attack on the senior German battleship *Tirpitz*, but fails to sink it.

Left: Indian Army officers report Japanese positions via radio during the Battle of Kohima, which starts on 4 April.

April 1944

Josef Goebbels becomes absolute ruler of Berlin on 7 April.

Tuesday 4: The Battle of Kohima, the decisive engagement for control of India, begins between Allied and Japanese forces.

Wednesday 5: Jews in occupied Hungary are ordered to wear yellow stars.

US Marines capture Utirik Atoll in the Marshal Islands.

Thursday 6: Actress and model Anita Pallenberg is born in Rome, Italy (died 2017).

Friday 7: Josef Goebbels is appointed absolute ruler of Berlin by Hitler.

Saturday 8: The USSR's Jassy-Kishinev Offensive (the invasion of Romania) begins.

The Battle of the Tennis Court takes place in Kohima as a small band of British, Indian and Gurkha troops halt the Japanese advance into India, holding out until 13 May against overwhelming odds. The battle is so called as much of it takes place around the tennis court of the local deputy commissioner.

Left: Soviet troops advance on Odessa in the Ukraine. The city is taken on 10 April.

April 1944

General Slim, Indian Army chief, with his wife Lady Slim. He oversees the repulse of Japanese forces on 10 April.

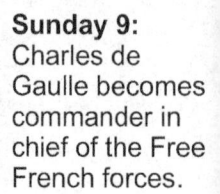

German prisoners are marched from Odessa after the city is captured on 10 April.

Sunday 9: Charles de Gaulle becomes commander in chief of the Free French forces.

Monday 10: Indian Army commander General Bill Slim orders a massive counter-attack to repel invading Japanese forces at Imphal and Kohima.

Soviet forces seize Odessa in the Crimea.

Tuesday 11: Soviet troops capture the Crimean towns of Dzankhoy and Kerch.

Wednesday 12: In the Battle of Targu Frumos, Axis forces successful repel the Soviet advance into Romania.

Thursday 13: As German forces retreat from the Crimea, the Soviets capture the region's second largest city, Simferopol.

Friday 14: 800 people are killed when a munitions ship, the SS *Fort Stikine*, explodes in Victoria Dock, Bombay.

Saturday 15: Soviet forces seize Tarnopol, Ukraine.

April 1944

Sunday 16: The first RAF air raids on Romania begin.

Monday 17: The Battle of Central Henan begins between Chinese and occupying Japanese forces in China.

Tuesday 18: Soviet troops capture Balaclava in the Crimea.

Wednesday 19: Allied forces attack Sabang in Japanese-held Indonesia.

Guy Lombardo tops the charts on 22 April.

Thursday 20: The RAF makes its largest attack of the war so far on Germany, dropping 4500 tons of bombs in one night.

Friday 21: French Algerian women are given the vote.

670 people are killed in an Allied air raid on German-occupied Paris.

Saturday 22: Hitler and Mussolini meet to discuss the deteriorating situation in German-occupied Italy.

It's Love-love-love by Guy Lombardo and his Orchestra tops the US charts.

Right: Fred MacMurray and Barbara Stanwyck star in the film noir classic *Double Indemnity*, released on 24 April.

April 1944

British secret agent Patrick Leigh Fermor kidnaps a senior German officer on 26 April.

Sunday 23: US troops capture the island of Hollandia in New Guinea.

Monday 24: The film-noir thriller *Double Indemnity* starring Fred MacMurray and Barbara Stanwyck is released.

Tuesday 25: German forces occupying Hungary suggest the 'blood for goods' deal, offering the Allies one million Jewish refugees in exchange for foreign goods. The Allies refuse to support the deal.

Ballroom dancer Len Goodman is born in Wolverhampton.

Wednesday 26: A team of British special agents and Greek resistance fighters led by travel writer Patrick Leigh Fermor kidnap Heinrich Kreipe, commander of German forces in occupied Crete. The incident is later made into the film *Ill Met by Moonlight*.

Michael Fish is born on 27 April.

Thursday 27: BBC TV weatherman Michael Fish, famous for denying the approach of the 1987 hurricane in southern England, is born in Sussex.

All non-vital civilian travel abroad is banned by the British government as the build up to D-Day begins.

US Army memorial at Slapton Sands, Devon, commemorating the sacrifice of 28 April.

April 1944

The first prefabs are shown to the British public on 30 April.

Friday 28: 749 American soldiers are killed at Slapton Sands, Devon, when German submarines attack Exercise Tiger, the first major rehearsal for the D-Day landings.

Saturday 29: The Canadian destroyer HMCS *Athabaskan* is sunk in the English Channel.

Sunday 30: The first prefabricated homes or 'prefabs' go on display in London. The system-built bungalows are intended as a quick and cheap solution for bombed-out families.

May 1944

Monday 1: 200 Greek communists are executed by occupying German forces in Athens as a reprisal against the killing of a German general.

Tuesday 2: In a secret deal with Britain and the USA, neutral Spain agrees to halt exports of tungsten to Germany. The metal, used in arms manufacture, is in global short supply.

Wednesday 3: Soemu Toyada is made commander in chief of the Imperial Japanese Fleet.

Exercise Fabius, the 'full dress rehearsal' for the D-Day landings, takes place on the south coast of England.

Thursday 4: The Bing Crosby film *Going My Way* opens in the USA.

Friday 5: The thriller film *Gaslight,* starring Charles Boyer and Ingrid Bergman, is released in the USA. The film, which inspires the term 'gaslighting' to describe a deliberately turning someone mad, also sees the first screen appearance of *Murder She Wrote* star Angela Lansbury.

Saturday 6: Mahatma Gandhi is released by British authorities after two

Bing Crosby.

May 1944

Gaslight is released on 5 May.

years of house arrest.

The Biltmore Conference opens in New York City, to discuss an official Zionist policy on Palestine.

I Love You by Bing Crosby tops the US music charts.

Sunday 7: A USAF 1,500 bomber raid on Berlin takes place.

Monday 8: The Czechoslovak government in exile in London agrees to the Soviet liberation of their country.

Tuesday 9: The world's first eye bank for corneal transplants is opened in New York City.

Wednesday 10: Aleksandr Vasilevsky, chief of the Soviet general staff, is injured when his car hits a land mine.

Thursday 11: Allied forces stage heavy air raids in the Calais region of France, to deceive the Germans into thinking that will be the landing site for D-Day.

The drama film *The White Cliffs of Dover* starring Irene Dunne and Alan Marshal is released.

Friday 12: Sepoy Kamal Ram, 19, of the Indian Army, single-handedly wipes out three German machine gun posts on the Gustav Line in Italy, for which action he later receives the Victoria Cross.

Sepoy Kamal Ram receives the Victoria Cross in July 1944 from HM King George VI for his action on 12 May.

May 1944

Captain Richard Wakeford, 22, receives the Victoria Cross from HM King George VI for taking 20 prisoners at Monte Cassino on 13 May while armed only with a revolver.

The author Max Brand, creator of 'Dr Kildare' is killed aged 51 while working as a war correspondent in Italy.

The author and critic Sir Arthur Quiller-Couch dies aged 80.

Saturday 13: At Kohima, the Battle of the Tennis Court ends in victory for the Allies as invading Japanese forces are pushed back from the Indian border.

Richard Wakeford, a 22-year old temporary captain in the Hampshire Regiment, storms a German position at Monte Cassino, Italy and takes 20 prisoners, while armed only with a revolver. For this action he later receives the Victoria Cross.

Sunday 14: The novel *Strange Fruit* by Lilian Smith hits number one in the New York Times Bestseller list.

Lilian Smith's critique of US racial segregation, *Strange Fruit*, tops the New York Times bestseller list on 14 May.

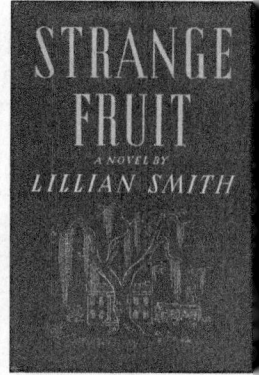

May 1944

Star Wars director George Lucas is born in Modesto, California.

Monday 15: British commandos begin Operation Tarbrush, a series of raids on the French coast to gain intelligence for the D-Day landings.

Tuesday 16: The Japanese submarine I-176 is sunk off Papua New Guinea by the US Navy.

Wednesday 17: Allied forces begin the Siege of Myitkyina against the Japanese in Burma.

George Lucas is born on 14 May.

Thursday 18: The Battle of Monte Cassino in Italy ends in Allied victory after 123 days as German forces abandon their positions.

Friday 19: The German submarine U-960 is sunk in the Mediterranean.

Saturday 20: The singer Joe Cocker is born in Sheffield, Yorkshire.

Polish resistance capture an intact V2 rocket and dismantle it, sending the components to London for analysis.

The ruins of Monte Cassino after the German retreat of 18 May.

May 1944

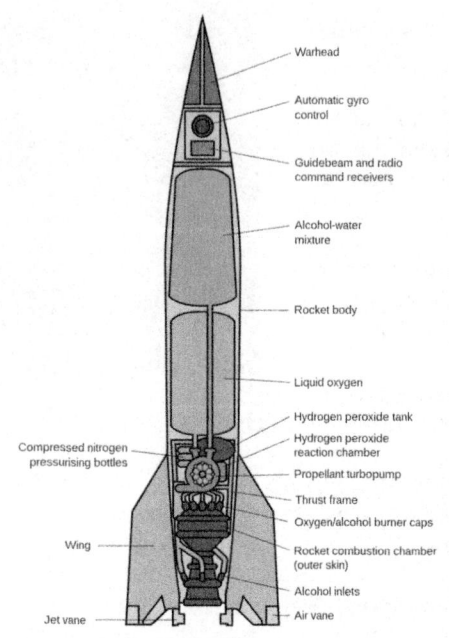

Labels on V2 rocket diagram: Warhead; Automatic gyro control; Guidebeam and radio command receivers; Alcohol-water mixture; Rocket body; Liquid oxygen; Hydrogen peroxide tank; Hydrogen peroxide reaction chamber; Compressed nitrogen pressurising bottles; Propellant turbopump; Thrust frame; Oxygen/alcohol burner caps; Wing; Rocket combustion chamber (outer skin); Alcohol inlets; Jet vane; Air vane.

Above: Hitler's deadliest weapon, the V2 rocket. Polish resistance manage to capture and dismantle one of the missiles on 20 May, smuggling the components to London for analysis.

Sunday 21: 163 die in a fire on board a landing craft at Pearl Harbor during exercises for the US invasion of the Mariana Islands.

Mary Robinson, first female President of the Republic of Ireland, is born in Ballina, County Mayo.

Monday 22: The Japanese destroyer *Asanagi* is sunk off Peel Island in the Pacific.

Tuesday 23: In a referendum, the people of Iceland vote for independence from Denmark.

Wednesday 24: Allied troops breach the Hitler Line in central Italy as the push north to Austria picks up speed.

Thursday 25: The puppeteer Frank Oz (*The Muppet Show*) is born in Hereford, England.

Friday 26: Allied forces come within 70 miles of Rome as the Italian cities of Cori and San Giovani are captured.

Saturday 27: The Battle of Biak begins in New Guinea.

Sunday 28: Rudy Giulani, Mayor of New York City, is born in Brooklyn, New York.

Rudy Giulani.

May 1944

Singer Gladys Knight is born in Atlanta, Georgia.

Monday 29: The 'Baby Blitz', the last major aerial bombing campaign of the war by conventional German aircraft, is called off after five months of attacks on southeast England.

Tuesday 30: Éamon de Valera's Fianna Fáil party wins the general election in Eire.

Princess Charlotte of Monaco abdicates in favour of her son, Prince Rainier.

Mary Robinson is born on 21 May.

Wednesday 31: The Government of India announces the formation of the Department of Planning and Development for the postwar period.

Members of London's Blitz Repair Team patch up damage to bombed houses, spring 1944. The last major conventional air raids end on 29 May, but damage to buildings continues from V1 and V2 attacks.

June 1944

Thursday 1: Two US navy blimps complete the first crossing of the Atlantic by non-rigid airships.

The actor Robert Powell (*The 39 Steps, The Detectives*) is born in Salford, Lancashire.

Friday 2: Allied troops cross the Caesar Line, the last Axis defence of Rome; Hitler orders German forces to abandon the city.

Saturday 3: Albert Kesselring, head of German forces in Rome, declares the Italian capital an open city, meaning that no force should be used in its capture.

Above: Hans Asperger discovers Asperger's Syndrome on 3 June

Asperger Syndrome is first identified by Austrian doctor Hans Asperger.

Sunday 4: Rome becomes the first Axis capital to fall to the Allies. Retreating German troops disobey Hitler's order to destroy all bridges on the Tiber.

RAF meteorologist Group Captain James Stagg, after analysing weather reports, successfully recommends that D-Day be postponed from 5 to 6 June.

June 1944

Rome is liberated without contest by Allied forces on 4 June, and troops are soon able to safely tour the city.

Left: British and American soldiers in St Peter's Square. Above: an Italian woman inspects the quality of a soldier's kilt at the Colosseum.

Monday 5: Pope Pius XII gives an open air service in St Peter's Basilica giving thanks for the liberation of Rome.
The Battle of Anzio ends in Allied victory after 136 days.

Tuesday 6: Operation Overlord (D-Day): the largest invasion in history begins as 160,000 Allied troops cross the English Channel to land in Normandy, opening the Second Front.

Wednesday 7: Actress Judy Garland divorces songwriter husband David Rose.

The Battle of Breville begins after Allied forces successfully establish a bridgehead in Normandy.

Thursday 8: The pro-Allied leader of Italy, Pietro Badoglio, moves his government to Rome.

Gregory Peck makes his feature film debut in *Days of Glory*.

Friday 9: The Italian cities of Tarquinia and Viterbo are captured by the US Fifth Army.

June 1944

Left: US troops storm the beaches at Normandy at dawn on 6 June.

Below: Germans are taken prisoner by British troops on D-Day.

Saturday 10: 642 French civilians are murdered by German troops in the Oradour-sur-Glane massacre, one of the worst outrages of the war; on the same day 214 civilians are massacred in Distomo, Greece, in retaliation for partisan attacks on occupying German forces.

Joe Nuxhall of the Cincinatti Reds makes his debut as the youngest major league baseball player to this date, aged 15.

Sunday 11: US troops capture the towns of Carentan and Lison in Normandy.

Monday 12: US President Franklin Roosevelt gives his 30th and final 'fireside chat' speech on the radio.

British and American troops convene at Carentan to form a 50 mile-long battlefront in Normandy.

June 1944

The first V1 bombs attack London on 13 June.

Above: civil defence workers listen for survivors after a V1 attack in London.

Tuesday 13: Six people are killed when the first V1 flying bombs attack southern England. The pilotless craft, known as 'buzz bombs' or 'doodlebugs', are soon being sent over at the rate of dozens a day. Travelling at high speed, no warning of attack is possible other than listening for the 'cut out' as the engine stops, indicating the bomb is about to hit.

Wednesday 14: Charles de Gaulle, leader of the Free French forces, visits the Normany beach-head.

An RAF Mosquito plane records the first successful shooting down of a V1 flying bomb.

Thursday 15: The United States Air Force bombs Yawata, the first attack on the Japanese home islands.

The Battle of Saipan begins in the Pacific.

Right: Charles de Gaulle meets British commander Field Marshal 'Monty' Montgomery in France on 14 June.

June 1944

Ivanoe Bonomi becomes Italian PM on 18 June.

Ray Davies (shown here in 1967) is born on 21 June.

Friday 16: The Treaty of Vis is signed in Yugoslavia, in an attempt to merge the Yugoslav government-in-exile with communist partisans.

Saturday 17: Iceland formally declares independence from Denmark.

Sunday 18: 121 people are killed when a V1 flying bomb hits the Guards Chapel in London, during Sunday service.

Ivanoe Bonomi replaces Pietro Badoglio as Prime Minister of Italy.

Monday 19: Major partisan attacks erupt in German-occupied Belarus, as the Soviets begin Operation Bagration, the eastern-front counterpart to the D-Day landings.

Tuesday 20: Hitler's new secret weapon, the V2 rocket, becomes the first powered man-made object to reach space, during a test launch from Germany.

Wednesday 21: Ray Davies, lead singer of the Kinks, is born in Muswell Hill, London.

Thursday 22: The Japanese invasion of India is finally thwarted as British and Indian Army forces are victorious in the Battle of Kohima.

Friday 23: Corporal Sefanaia Sukanaivalu of the Fiji Infantry Regiment is killed by enemy fire while rescuing wounded comrades in Bouganville, Solomon Islands. He is later awarded a posthumous Victoria Cross, the only Fijian to have received that honour.

Saturday 24: German forces launch the new Mistel unmanned bomber drone.

June 1944

Left: German commanders of Cherbourg surrender to Maj-Gen Joseph Collins, US Army, on 26 June.

Guitarist Jeff Beck is born in Wallington, Surrey.

Sunday 25: The Battle of Tali-Ihantala between Finnish and Soviet forces begins; it is the largest military confrontation in Nordic history.

Monday 26: German forces at Cherbourg surrender.

Tuesday 27: The US government passes the Veterans' Preference Act requiring demobbed servicemen to be given priority for civilian jobs.

Wednesday 28: Phillipe Henriot, Vichy France's Secretary of State for Information and Propaganda, is assassinated by the French Resistance.

Thursday 29: The dance band singer Chick Henderson, of the Joe Loss Band, is killed in action aged 31.

Friday 30: The First Battle of the Odon, the action to capture the French city of Caen, begins.

Jeff Beck is born on 24 June.

July 1944

Saturday 1: The United Nations Monetary and Financial Conference begins in Bretton Woods, New Hampshire to set global postwar financial policy.

I'll Be Seeing You by Bing Crosby hits number one in the US charts.

Sunday 2: W. Somerset Maugham's novel *The Razor's Edge* tops the *New York Times* bestseller list.

Monday 3: Minsk, capital of Belarus and the last German occupied city on Soviet soil, is captured by the Red Army.

Tuesday 4: To celebrate American independence day, all artillery units in the US First Army are ordered to fire one round towards German lines at precisely mid-day.

A Soviet soldier is greeted by civilians in Minsk on 3 July.

July 1944

A poster for *The Mummy's Ghost*, starring Lon Chaney, released on 7 July.

Wednesday 5: Canadian troops seize the city of Carpiquet in Normandy.

Thursday 6: Polish resistance fighters begin an armed uprising against German occupying forces in Wilno (now Vilnius).

Admiral Miklos Horthy, Regent of Hungary, orders an end to the deportation of his country's Jews to concentration camps.

Friday 7: The horror film *The Mummy's Ghost* starring Lon Chaney Jr is released.

The last Japanese *banzai* (suicide) charge takes place against US forces in the Battle of Saipan.

Saturday 8: German forces begin the liquidation of the Kovno Ghetto in Kaunus, Lithuania.

Highland infantry take a well-earned tea break after the capture of Caen on 9 July.

July 1944

The German Tiger II tank is first used on 11 July.

Sunday 9: After fierce resistance, British and Canadian troops capture the French city of Caen.

Monday 10: A second evacuation of London begins as 41,000 mothers and children leave to escape attacks by V1 flying bombs.

Tuesday 11: The German heavy Tiger II tank goes into action for the first time, in France.

Wednesday 12: Brigadier General Theodore Roosevelt Jr, son of President Theodore Roosevelt and senior commander of US forces in Normandy, dies of natural causes while on active service in France.

Thursday 13: Erno Rubik, inventor of Rubik's Cube, is born in Budapest, Hungary.

Friday 14: The Polish resistance in Wilno (Vilnius) suffer a Pyhrric victory – they defeat the occupying German forces but are then arrested by newly arrived Soviet troops.

Saturday 15: Actor Jan-Michael Vincent (*Airwolf*) is born in Denver, Colorado (died 2019).

Sunday 16: Adolf Hitler leaves his Alpine retreat of Berchtesgaden for the last time as he moves to his eastern front headquarters at the Wolf's Lair.

Monday 17: Senior German officer Field Marshall Erwin Rommel is invalided out of the war when his staff car is shot at by a Royal Canadian Airforce Spitfire pilot near Livarot, France.

July 1944

Tuesday 18: The British artist Rex Whistler is killed on active service in France, aged 39.

Wednesday 19: The Italian city of Leghorn (Livorno) is captured by the US Fifth Army.

Thursday 20: A bomb plot to assassinate Adolf Hitler, led by Colonel Claus Von Stauffenberg, ends in failure. The meeting room at the Wolf's Lair headquarters is badly damaged but Hitler escapes almost unscathed. Following the attack he is able to meet with Italy's Benito Mussolini as planned; it is the last meeting between the two dictators.

Self-portrait of the artist Rex Whistler, who dies on 18 July.

Friday 21: Adolf Hitler makes a broadcast on German radio assuring the populace that he is still alive; troops pour in to Berlin to round up the assassination attempt conspirators; several are later tortured and executed.

Hitler and Mussolini examine bomb damage following the assassination attempt of 20 July.

July 1944

Saturday 22: Majdanek concentration camp in Poland becomes the first camp to be liberated by the Allies.

Sunday 23: An armed uprising by the Polish resistance begins against German occupying forces.

Monday 24: The French city of Saint Lo is captured by Allied forces.

Tuesday 25: The Battle of Tannenberg Line begins on the eastern front.

Wednesday 26: Reza Shah, the deposed monarch of Persia, dies aged 66.

Top: the RAF Gloster Meteor is launched on 27 July. Above: The Messerschmitt M163 Komet goes into service on 28 July.

Thursday 27: The Gloster Meteor, the first RAF jet fighter and the only Allied jet aircraft of the war, goes into service with 616 Squadron RAF.

Friday 28: Germany's Messerschmitt Me163 Komet goes into service; it remains the only rocket-powered fighter aircraft to have been used in combat.

Saturday 29: 'Black Friday'; 39 RAF Lancaster bombers are shot down during a raid on Stuttgart, Germany.

Sunday 30: British troops in Normandy begin 'Operation Bluecoat' to capture the towns of Vire and Mont Pincon.

Monday 31: Antoine de Saint-Exupéry, pilot and author of the children's classic *The Little Prince*, is killed on active service in France aged 44.

August 1944

Tuesday 1: The Warsaw Uprising by the Polish resistance against German occupation forces by begins.

Wednesday 2: 100 V1 flying bombs land on London; Tower Bridge is one of the buildings which sustains damage.

Thursday 3: The 1944 Education Act receives Royal Assent. The Act sets up the postwar system of the Eleven Plus examination and the division of schools into Grammar, Secondary Modern and Technical.

Left: a partisan in Florence.

Far left: the ruins of the Ponte Alle Grazia, destroyed in the German retreat from Florence on 4 August.

August 1944

Teenage diarist Anne Frank is arrested on 4 August.

Friday 4: German forces retreat from Florence, destroying all the city's historic bridges except the medieval Ponte Vecchio.

German police find the young Jewish diarist Anne Frank hiding in an attic in Amsterdam; she is deported to a concentration camp.

Saturday 5: 231 Japanese prisoners of war are killed in a mass breakout of Cowra POW camp in New South Wales, Australia; all escapees are recaptured within ten days.

Swinging on a Star by Bing Crosby hits number one in the US charts.

Sunday 6: Soviet forces begin the Osovets Offensive against German forces in Belarus.

Monday 7: The Battle for Brest begins in northern France.

The IBM Harvard Mk1 electro-mechanical computer goes into operation in the USA.

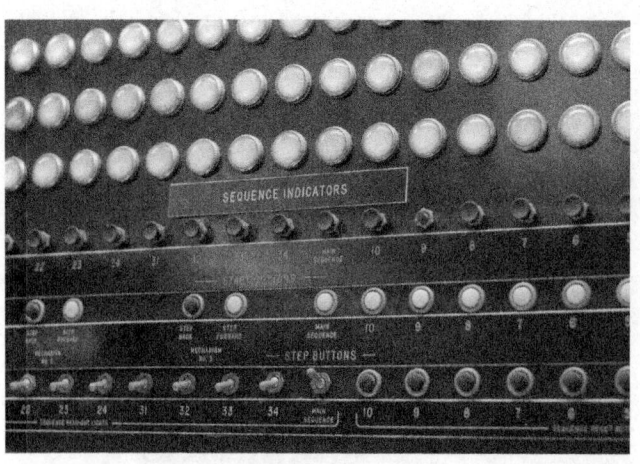

The switchboard of the IBM Harvard Mk1 computer, which goes into use on 7 August.

August 1944

Germany's high-tech jet bomber, the Junkers Ju287, makes its first test flight on 8 August. The war ends before it can go into mass production.

Tuesday 8: The Junkers Ju287 German jet bomber makes its first flight.

Wednesday 9: The Free French provisional government declares the law of the French republic to apply in France, nullifying the laws of the German puppet Vichy government.

Thursday 10: US forces are victorious in the Battle of Guam in the Pacific.

Friday 11: Actor Ian McDiarmid (Lord Darth Sidious in *Star Wars*) is born in Carnoustie, Forfarshire.

Saturday 12: The Battle of the Falaise Pocket, the decisive engagement of the Battle of Normandy, begins.

The Allied invasion fleet reaches the southern French coast on 15 August.

August 1944

Above: Marshal Petain, leader of France's pro-German Vichy Government, is arrested on 20 August.

German communist leader Ernst Thalmann is executed on 18 August.

The first undersea oil pipeline is laid between England and France.

Sunday 13: Soviet troops capture Voru and Valga in Estonia.

Monday 14: Operation Tractable, the final offensive of the Battle of Normandy, begins.

Tuesday 15: Operation Dragoon begins as Allied forces open a second invasion front on France's Mediterranean coast.

Wednesday 16: American troops liberate the French city of Chartres.

Thursday 17: Allied forces capture the French towns of St Malo and Falaise.

Friday 18: Ernst Thalmann, 58, leader of the German Communist Party is executed at Buchenwald concentration camp.

18,000 prisoners are taken by the Allies as the German army retreats eastward over the River Orne in France.

Saturday 19: As the Allies approach the French capital, the first shots are fired by French resistance snipers on German troops in Paris.

Sunday 20: Marshal Petain, leader of France's puppet Vichy regime, is arrested by occupying German forces.

Bob Hamilton wins the 26th PGA golf tournament in Spokane, Washington.

August 1944

Monday 21: The Dumbarton Oaks Conference begins in Washington, DC, to discuss the establishment of the United Nations.

Allied forces are victorious in the Battle of the Falaise Pocket in France.

The comedy-drama film *A Canterbury Tale* starring Dennis Price and Sheila Sim is released in the UK.

Tuesday 22: German troops on the Greek island of Crete begin destroying villages and massacring civilians.

The drama film *Kismet* starring Ronald Colman and Marlene Dietrich is released.

King Michael of Romania leads a coup on 23 August.

Wednesday 23: A military coup in Romania led by King Michael I overthrows the pro-German government of Ion Antonescu.

General de Gaulle makes his triumphant entry into Paris on 25 August.

August 1944

Left: a French partisan, a US Army officer and two gendarmes attempt to flush out a sniper during the liberation of Marseille on 29 August.

Abdulmejid II, last Caliph of the Ottoman Empire, dies aged 76.

Thursday 24: Canadian forces capture Bernay, France.

Friday 25: General Dietrich von Choltitz, commander of the German garrison in Paris, surrenders the city to Allied forces. At 4pm General Charles de Gaulle enters the capital where he is greeted by huge crowds.

Romania changes sides, declaring war on Germany.

Allied forces begin using the 'Red Ball Express' military convoy system, with express roads closed to all other traffic.

Saturday 26: The French city of Toulon is liberated by Allied forces.

General de Gaulle attends a victory parade and service at Notre Dame cathedral in Paris; the event is disrupted by sniper fire from the last few remaining pro-German fighters.

Abdulmedjid II, the last of the Caliphs (global Muslim leaders) dies on 23 August.

Sunday 27: Operation Doppelkopf, the German counter-offensive in Latvia, is partially successful.

August 1944

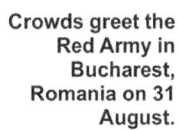

Crowds greet the Red Army in Bucharest, Romania on 31 August.

Monday 28: Soviet forces successfully push German troops back from Belarus in the Kaunas Offensive.

Tuesday 29: Free French forces liberate Marseille.

The administration of Paris is handed over from the Allies to the French Committee of National Liberation under General de Gaulle.

Wednesday 30: The Soviet Union refuses to accept Bulgaria's declaration of neutrality.

Thursday 31: Occupying German forces surrender the Romanian capital of Bucharest to the Red Army.

Left: as Allied supply lines across France grow longer, the Red Ball Express system is set up on 25 August. Here a US military policeman directs high-speed convoys on a route restricted to civilians.

September 1944

Friday 1: Canadian forces capture Dieppe, France.

The black comedy film *Arsenic and Old Lace* starring Cary Grant and Peter Lorre premieres in New York City.

Saturday 2: Finland breaks off diplomatic relations with Germany and orders all Germans to leave the country.

Sunday 3: The British Second Army liberates Brussels.

Monday 4: Hostilities cease between Soviet and Finnish forces in Finland.

Tuesday 5: The Soviet Union declares war on Bulgaria, which although not formally part of the Axis was considered a close ally.

Wednesday 6: Polish forces liberate Ypres in Belgium.

Left: jubilant crowds pile on to a British army lorry as Brussels is liberated on 3 September.

September 1944

In Britain, blackout restrictions are relaxed and duty for the Home Guard (civilian militia) becomes voluntary.

Thursday 7: Hungary declares war on Romania and sends troops into the disputed border territory of Transylvania.

Friday 8: The Belgian government in exile returns to Brussels from London.

A Free Dutch officer greets civilians in newly liberated Brussels, 3 September.

The first German V2 rocket lands on London. There is no way of stopping or warning against the missiles, and the authorities keep their existence secret until November.

Saturday 9: A coup d'etat in Bulgaria takes place by the pro-Soviet Fatherland Front.

Sunday 10: Luxembourg is liberated by Allied forces.

A Luxembourg flag flies from a damaged building as the tiny state is liberated on 10 September.

Monday 11: A provisional communist government is set up in Poland under Boleslaw Bierut.

Sgt Warner Holzinger of the US Cavalry is said to be the first Allied soldier to cross into Germany when he leads a reconnaisance party over the border from Luxembourg.

September 1944

Tuesday 12: Romania signs an armistice with the Allies in Moscow and agrees to supply troops to fight Germany.

Canadian forces capture Le Havre, France.

Wednesday 13: The cartoonist W Heath Robinson, known for his drawings of elaborate fantastical machinery, dies aged 72.

Thursday 14: Canadian and British troops break through the Gothic Line in Italy.

Friday 15: The Great Atlantic Hurricane hits the US eastern seaboard.

Saturday 16: Soviet forces occupy Sofia, capital of Bulgaria.

A transport strike begins in occupied Denmark in protest over the transfer of political prisoners to Germany.

Sunday 17: Operation Market Garden, also known as the Battle of Arnhem, begins in the Netherlands.

Blackout restrictions are further relaxed in London.

Monday 18: One of the worst disasters of the war occurs when the Japanese ship *Junyo Maru* is sunk off the coast of Sumatra with the loss of 5620 lives, mostly British prisoners of war.

Left: Danish civilians form barricades in Copenhagen in protest against German occupation; a state of emergency is declared on 19 September.

September 1944

Left: US airborne troops receive a final briefing before embarking on the doomed Operation Market Garden on 25 September.

Tuesday 19: Occupying German forces in Denmark order the disarming of the Danish police and declare a state of emergency as their grip on the country loosens.

Wednesday 20: The tiny European state of San Marino is liberated by Allied forces.

The pirate film *Frenchman's Creek* starring Joan Fontaine and Arturo de Cordova is released.

Thursday 21: Allied forces liberate Rimini in Italy.

Friday 22: Canadian troops seize Bolougne, France.

Michael Douglas is born on 25 September.

Saturday 23: Soviet forces enter Hungary.

Sunday 24: British troops capture Deurne in the Netherlands.

Monday 25: Operation Market Garden, the attempt at establishing an Allied bridgehead into Germany via the Netherlands, ends in defeat. The battle is later made the subject of the film *A Bridge Too Far*.

Actor Michael Douglas is born in New Brunswick, New Jersey.

September 1944

A soldier of 1st Btn The Jewish Brigade, formed as part of the British Army on 28 September. The shell is inscribed with the message 'A gift for Hitler'.

Tuesday 26: Greek resistance groups agree to acknowledge the authority of the Greek Government in Exile.

TV presenter Anne Robinson is born in Crosby, Lancashire.

Wednesday 27: Soviet troops enter Albania.

The US evangelist Aimee Semple McPherson dies aged 53.

Thursday 28: Prime Minister Winston Churchill announces the formation of a Jewish brigade for the British Army, to be recruited from British Mandatory Palestine (now Israel).

Friday 29: Soviet troops begin the Baltic Offensive to clear the Baltic islands of occupying German forces.

Saturday 30: Calais falls to the Canadian Army.

October 1944

Sunday 1: The St Louis Browns beat the New York Yankees 5-2 to win baseball's American League.

Monday 2: The Warsaw Uprising by Polish resistance is put down after two months by occupying German forces.

Tuesday 3: Five partisans are killed during a botched attempt to kidnap a leading Italian fascist, Guido Buffarini Guidi, at Lake Como.

Wednesday 4: The first Allied bombing raid takes place on Prague, capital of German-occupied Czechoslovakia.

Thursday 5: The first incidence of a jet fighter being shot down by piston-engined aircraft takes place when RCAF pilots down a German Messerschmitt Me62 over Holland.

The stage musical *Bloomer Girl* opens on Broadway.

Friday 6: As the Red Army approaches, the leader of Serbia's German puppet government, Milan Nedic, flees to Austria.

The Battle of Debrecen begins in Hungary's second city.

Saturday 7: A mass breakout attempt takes place in Auschwitz concentration camp; 200 are killed and all escapees are eventually recaptured.

October 1944

The Mills Brothers top the US charts on 7 October.

You Always Hurt The One You Love by the Mills Brothers hits number one in the US singles charts.

Sunday 8: US forces are victorious in the Battle of Crucifix Hill, the first major engagement by Allied forces within the borders of Germany.

Monday 9: The Allied leaders begin the Fourth Moscow Conference.

The St Louis Cardinals defeat the St Louis Browns 3-1 to win the 1944 baseball World Series.

Tuesday 10: Ramon Grau becomes President of Cuba.

The Italian Resistance has its largest victory when it captures the city of Alba in Piedmont.

Wednesday 11: Hungary makes a secret peace deal with the USSR and agrees to change sides and declare war on Germany.

The mystery film *Laura* starring Gene Tierney and Dana Andrews is released.

The thriller film *To Have And Have Not* starring Humphrey Bogart and Lauren Bacall (in her screen debut) is released.

Thursday 12: Canadian explorer Henry Larsen makes the first sea crossing in one season of the

Lauren Bacall and Humphrey Bogart in *To Have And Have Not*, released on 11 October.

October 1944

British troops in Athens following its liberation on 13 October.

Northwest Passage through the Arctic.

Friday 13: Allied forces liberate Athens from German occupation.

Saturday 14: Germany's Field Marshall Erwin Rommel commits suicide aged 52 following revelations of his involvement in the plot to assassinate Hitler.

Sunday 15: Admiral Miklos Horthy, Regent of Hungary, announces his surrender to the Allies; German forces immediately arrest him and install a puppet government under Ferenc Szalasi.

Monday 16: Italy's Gothic Line is overcome as the US Army and Indian Army push northwards towards Bologna.

Tuesday 17: The American recapture of the Japanese-occupied Phillippines begins as General Douglas MacArthur's forces land at Leyte.

Wednesday 18: The *Volkssturm* (German Home Guard) is raised for national defence, conscripting men who are too old, young or unfit to serve in the regular forces.

Thursday 19: 300 die when a hurricane hits Sarasota, Florida.

Right: Hungary's leader Admiral Horthy is arrested by the Germans on 15 October.

October 1944

Left: the *Volkssturm* (German Home Guard) is formed on 18 October; here a member trains with an anti-tank rifle.

Friday 20: General Douglas MacArthur broadcasts a radio message to the people of the Philippines, fulfilling his promise of 1942, 'I will return'. He states simply 'I have returned.'

Belgrade, capital of Yugoslavia, is captured by Soviet forces.

Saturday 21: Aachen becomes the first major German city to capitulate to Allied forces.

Sunday 22: The Battle of Angaur in the Pacific ends in US victory.

Monday 23: One of the largest naval engagements in history takes place when the US Navy and Royal Australian Navy clash with Japanese forces in the Leyte Gulf, Phillippines.

Tuesday 24: Soviet forces seize German-occupied Riga, capital of Latvia.

Wednesday 25: The first Kamikaze (Japanese suicide bomber) attack of the war takes place in the Battle of Leyte Gulf, Phillipines, as the aircraft carrier USS *St Lo* is sunk.

Thursday 26: HRH Princess Beatrice, the youngest and longest-lived of Queen Victoria's children, dies aged 87.

William Temple, Archbishop of Canterbury, dies aged 63.

Friday 27: German troops push back a major Soviet offensive in East Prussia.

October 1944

General Douglas Macarthur, US Army, wades ashore during the liberation of the Phillippines on 20 October.

Saturday 28: Bulgaria signs an armistice with the Allies.

General de Gaulle orders the French Resistance to disarm.

Sunday 29: NBC radio broadcasts the first Jewish religious service to be held in Aachen, the first major German city to be occupied by Allied forces.

Monday 30: British troops capture the Italian city of Forli.

Tuesday 31: German forces evacuate Thessaloniki, Greece's second city, and scuttle all *Kriegsmarine* vessels.

Hundreds of German prisoners are marched through Aachen, which on 21 October becomes the first German city to fall to the Allies.

November 1944

The first *Fu-Go* Japanese intercontinental balloon bombs are launched against the USA on 3 November. Left: workers prepare a balloon bomb for launch.

Wednesday 1: A constitutional crisis erupts in Canada as the government disagrees on whether to enact military conscription.

The Mary Chase play *Harvey,* later made into a film with James Stewart, opens on Broadway.

Thursday 2: Marshal Tito becomes Prime Minister of Yugoslavia.

November 1944

Above: Democrat Party supporters canvassing in New York City for Franklin D Roosevelt, who wins a historic fourth term as US President on 7 November.

A forced deportation of Jews from Hungary begins; prior to German occupation there had been only limited anti-semitic legislation in the country.

Friday 3: Japan begins the *Fu-Go* (high altitude incendiary balloons) campaign against the US eastern seaboard.

Saturday 4: Australian forces land on the Japanese-held island of New Britain.

Sunday 5: British troops capture the Italian city of Ravenna.

Monday 6: The new government of Italy announces the raising of an army to fight on the Allied side.

All anti-semitic laws in France are struck down.

Lord Moyne, Britain's minister for the Middle East, is assassinated by Zionists in Cairo.

Tuesday 7: Franklin D Roosevelt is elected for an unprecedented fourth term in the US Presidential elections.

November 1944

Wednesday 8: The British government officially acknowledges the existence of the V2 rocket attacks on London, ending weeks of rumour and speculation.

Thursday 9: German forces on Walcheren Island in the Netherlands surrender.

Friday 10: The Allies recognise the new government of Albania under partisan leader Enva Hoxha.

The two year long musicians' strike in the USA comes to an end.

Saturday 11: The last German troops leave Greece.

Sunday 12: The RAF sinks the pride of the German fleet, the battleship *Tirpitz*, off the coast of Norway.

Kathleen Winsor's novel *Forever Amber* hits number one in the New York Times bestseller lists.

Monday 13: The first civil air service since 1939 begins in London.

Tuesday 14: Albanian partisans seize German occupied Durres, the country's second city.

A British sailor chalks a message on a torpedo intended for the *Tirpitz*; the battleship is finally sunk on 12 November.

November 1944

Wednesday 15: The war film *Thirty Seconds Over Tokyo* starring Spencer Tracy and Van Johnson is released.

Thursday 16: US forces begin an assault on Germany's defensive Siegfried Line.

Friday 17: The actor Danny DeVito is born in Neptune Township, NJ.

Saturday 18: Superboy makes his first comic book appearance.

Danny DeVito is born on 17 November.

Sunday 19: British troops capture the town of Geilenkirchen on the German/Dutch border.

Monday 20: Adolf Hitler retreats westward, leaving his Wolf's Lair headquarters on the Eastern Front for the last time.

Blackout restrictions are lifted in London's Fleet Street, Strand and Piccadilly.

English author PG Wodehouse, resident in France, is arrested by British military police for making perceived pro-German speeches on French radio.

Tuesday 21: The French army captures the city of Belfort near the Swiss border.

Wednesday 22: The film *Henry V* starring Laurence Olivier is released.

The film *Meet Me In St Louis* starring Judy Garland is released.

Above: Margaret O'Brien and Judy Garland star in *Meet Me In St Louis*, released on 22 November.

Thursday 23: French troops liberate Strasbourg, leaving La Rochelle as the last major French city under German occupation.

November 1944

Partisan leader Enva Hoxha takes over Albania as occupying German forces are defeated on 29 November.

The government of Canada introduces military conscription.

Friday 24: Ferenc Szalasi's pro-German government flees the Hungarian capital Budapest, setting up a new headquarters in Sopron on the Austrian border.

Canadian conscripts mutiny after refusing to serve overseas.

Saturday 25: 168 people are killed in the worst V2 rocket attack of the war, when a missile hits a crowded branch of Woolworth's in New Cross, London.

Sunday 26: As Allied forces close in, Heinrich Himmler orders a cover-up of the deaths at Auschwitz concentration camp.

Monday 27: 70 people are killed in an accidental explosion at a munitions dump at RAF Fauld, Staffordshire.

Tuesday 28: The newly-liberated port of Antwerp goes back into operation.

Wednesday 29: Albania is officially liberated as all pro-German forces in the country are defeated.

The five-day mutiny in the Canadian army is ended.

Thursday 30: 23 people are killed in a V2 rocket attack on Shooter's Hill, south London. The attack, of no strategic importance, is probably a mistake – by sending false reports to Germany via a double agent, British intelligence is able to cause many V2 rockets to fall short in London's suburbs instead of its more populous centre.

December 1944

Friday 1: Bela Bartok's *Concerto for Orchestra* is first performed, at the Boston Symphony Hall.

Saturday 2: France's General de Gaulle meets Josef Stalin in Moscow.

Sunday 3: Britain's Home Guard, the volunteer force for men too old or young to serve in the regular army, is formally stood down as the possibility of a German invasion becomes negligible.

Monday 4: The bread ration in the occupied Netherlands is cut to two pounds per person per week.

Left: a Home Guard anti-aircraft gun crew. As German air raids cease and the possibility of invasion ends, the force is stood down on 3 December.

December 1944

The hurriedly produced Heinkel He62 jet fighter first flies on 6 December as part of a desperate German attempt to gain air superiority.

Dennis Wilson, lead singer of the Beach Boys is born in Inglewood, California, (died 1983).

Tuesday 5: Soviet troops capture Szigetvar in southern Hungary.

Wednesday 6: Germany's Heinkel He62 jet fighter goes into service.

Thursday 7: 1233 are killed when an earthquake hits Tonankai, Japan.

Nicolae Radescu becomes Romania's last prime minister before the Soviet takeover.

Friday 8: The heaviest air raid of the Pacific theatre takes place as the USAF attacks the island of Iwo Jima.

Saturday 9: The writer and comedian Neil Innes is born in Danbury, Essex (died 2019).

Sunday 10: The first Nobel Prizes since 1939 are awarded.

Monday 11: The Kia motor company is founded in Korea.

The singer Brenda Lee is born in Atlanta, Georgia.

Brenda Lee (shown here in 1977) is born on 11 December.

Tuesday 12: Field Marshal Harold Alexander is made supreme commander of Allied forces in the Mediterranean.

December 1944

Mickey Rooney and Elizabeth Taylor in *National Velvet*, released on 14 December.

Wednesday 13: The Russian painter Wassily Kandinsky dies aged 77.

Thursday 14: HMS *Aldenham* becomes the last Royal Navy destroyer of the war to be lost, when it is sunk by a mine off the Croatian coast.

The film *National Velvet* starring Mickey Rooney and Elizabeth Taylor is released.

Friday 15: Bandleader Glenn Miller is missing, presumed dead, when the plane in which he is travelling is lost in fog over the English Channel.

The film *House of Frankenstein* starring Boris Karloff and Lon Chaney Jr is released.

Saturday 16: The last major German counterattack of the war, the Ardennes Offensive (also known as the Battle of the Bulge) begins.

In Milan, Italian fascist leader Benito Mussolini makes his final speech as Allied forces close in on northern Italy.

Sunday 17: The US army activates the 509th Composite Group, the formation charged with the use of nuclear weapons.

The actor Bernard Hill is born in Blackley, Lancashire.

Monday 18: The first edition of the Parisian newspaper *Le Monde* is published.

Above: Glenn Miller is missing, presumed dead, when his plane disappears over the English Channel on 15 December.

December 1944

Above: a German soldier in heavy winter clothing during the Battle of the Bulge, which begins on 16 December.

Above: Archbishop Damaskinos becomes Regent of Greece on 30 December.

British troops in Greece begin an offensive against ELAS communist rebels.

Tuesday 19: Senior US Army commanders meet in Verdun to discuss the response to Germany's Ardennes Offensive, which threatens to push the Allied advance back to the French coast.

Wednesday 20: The Siege of Bastogne begins in Belgium.

Thursday 21: German forces seize the city of St Vith in Belgium.

The Walt Disney animated musical *The Three Caballeros* is released.

Friday 22: General Anthony McAuliffe, commander of US forces in Bastogne, responds to a German request for his surrender with a letter containing one word: 'NUTS!'

Saturday 23: *Don't Fence Me In* by Bing Crosby and the Andrews Sisters hits number one in the US singles charts.

Sunday 24: The German counter offensive, the Battle of the Bulge, reaches its further westward extent at Celles, Belgium.

42 people are killed when 50 V-1 flying bombs hit Manchester.

December 1944

Monday 25: British Prime Minister Winston Churchill arrives in newly-liberated Athens to broker a ceasefire in the civil war between rival partisan forces.

Tuesday 26: The Tennessee Williams play *The Glass Menagerie* opens at the Civic Theatre in Chicago.

Wednesday 27: Former Prime Minister David Lloyd George announces his retirement as an MP.

Above: Julie Haydon stars in *The Glass Menagerie*, which opens on 26 December.

Thursday 28: The German counteroffensive in the Ardennes begins to be pushed back by US forces.

The musical *On The Town* by Leonard Bernstein opens on Broadway, introducing the hit song *New York New York*.

Friday 29: Soviet and Romanian forces begin the Siege of Budapest.

Saturday 30: Archbishop Damaskinos of Athens is declared Regent of Greece in London by the exiled King George II.

General Leslie Groves, head of the Manhattan Project into atomic weapons, announces that a nuclear bomb will be ready for testing by summer 1945.

The Grumman F8F Bearcat.

Sunday 31: The provisional government of Hungary declares war on Germany.

The Grumman F8F Bearcat fighter enters service with the US Navy.

More titles from Montpelier Publishing

A Little Book of Limericks:
Funny Rhymes for all the Family
ISBN 9781511524124

Scottish Jokes: A Wee Book of
Clean Caledonian Chuckles
ISBN 9781495297366

The Old Fashioned Joke Book:
Gags and Funny Stories
ISBN 9781514261989

Non-Religious Funeral Readings:
Philosophy and Poetry for Secular
Services
ISBN 9781500512835

Large Print Jokes: Hundreds of
Gags in Easy-to-Read Type
ISBN 9781517775780

**Spiritual Readings for Funerals
and Memorial Services**
ISBN 9781503379329

Victorian Murder: True Crimes,
Confessions and Executions
ISBN 9781530296194

Large Print Prayers: A Prayer for
Each Day of the Month
ISBN 9781523251476

**A Little Book of Ripping Riddles
and Confounding Conundrums**
ISBN 9781505548136

Vinegar uses: over 150 ways to use
vinegar
ISBN 9781512136623

Large Print Wordsearch:
100 Puzzles in Easy-to-Read Type
ISBN 9781517638894

The Pipe Smoker's Companion
ISBN 9781500441401

The Book of Church Jokes
ISBN 9781507620632

Bar Mitzvah Notebook
ISBN 9781976007781

Jewish Jokes
ISBN 9781514845769

Large Print Address Book
ISBN 9781539820031

How to Cook Without a Kitchen:
Easy, Healthy and Low-Cost Meals
9781515340188

Large Print Birthday Book
ISBN 9781544670720

Retirement Jokes
ISBN 9781519206350

Take my Wife: Hilarious Jokes of
Love and Marriage
ISBN 9781511790956

Welsh Jokes: A Little Book of
Wonderful Welsh Wit
ISBN 9781511612241

1001 Ways to Save Money: Thrifty
Tips for the Fabulously Frugal!
ISBN 9781505432534

Order online from Amazon or from your local bookshop

Printed in Great Britain
by Amazon